I LOVE MY DAD

أحِبُّ أَبِي

Shelley Admont
Illustrated by Sonal Goyal and Sumit Sakhuja

First edition, 2017

Translated from English by Amal Mrissa

قامت بترجمة هذه القصّة من الإنجليزيّة: أمل مريصة

Arabic editing by Fatima Bekkouche

Library and Archives Canada Cataloguing in Publication Data

I Love My Dad (Arabic Bilingual Edition)/ Shelley Admont

ISBN: 978-1-5259-0485-1 paperback

ISBN: 978-1-5259-0486-8 hardcover

ISBN: 978-1-5259-0484-4 eBook

Please note that the Arabic and English versions of the story have been written to be as close as possible. However, in some cases they differ in order to accommodate nuances and fluidity of each language.

Although the author and the publisher have made every effort to ensure the accuracy and completeness of information contained in this book, we assume no responsibility for errors , inaccuracies, omission, inconsistency, or consequences from such information.

For those I love the most

لأحبائي

One summer day, Jimmy the little bunny and his two older brothers were riding their bicycles. Their dad sat in the backyard, reading a book.

في يَوْمٍ صَيْفِيٍّ جَمِيلٍ، كَانَ الْأَرْنَبُ الصَّغِيرُ "جِيمِي" وَ أَخَوَاهُ الْأَكْبَرَانِ يَقُودُونَ دَرَّاجَاتِهِمْ، بَيْنَمَا كَانَ وَالِدُهُمْ جَالِسًا فِي فِنَاءِ الْبَيْتِ يَقْرَأُ كِتَابًا.

The two older bunnies laughed loudly as they raced. Jimmy tried to catch up on his training wheel bike.

تَسَابَقَ الْأَرْنَبَانِ الْأَكْبَرَانِ وَ هُمَا يَضْحَكَانِ عَالِيًا، أَمَّا جِيمِي فَحَاوَلَ اللَّحَاقَ بِهِمَا عَلَى دَرَّاجَةِ التَّدْرِيبِ خَاصَّتِهِ.

"Hey, wait for me! I want to race too!" Jimmy shouted. But his brothers were too far away and his bike was too small.

صَاحَ جِيمِي: "تَمَهَّلَا... انْتَظِرَانِي ! أُرِيدُ أَنْ أَتَسَابَقَ مَعَكُمَا أَيْضًا !" وَ لَكِنَّ شَقِيقَيْه كَانَا بَعِيدَيْنِ عَنْهُ جِدًا، وَ دَرَّاجَتُهُ كَانَتْ صَغِيرَةً جِدًّا.

Soon his brothers returned, giggling to each other. "It's not fair," screamed Jimmy. "I want to ride your big bikes too."

و بعد وقتٍ قَصيرٍ، عَادَ شَقيقاهُ وَ هُمَا يَضْحَكَانِ لِبَعْضِهِما الْبَعْض. فَصاحَ جيمي: "هَذَا لَيْسَ عَدْلًا، أُريدُ أَنْ أَرْكَبَ دَرَّاجَتَيْكُمَا الكَبيرَتَيْنِ أَيْضًا."

"But Jimmy, you're too small," said his oldest brother.

فَقالَ الْأَخُ الْأَكْبَرُ: "و لَكِنَّكَ صَغيرٌ جِدًّا يَا جيمي."

"And you don't even know how to ride a two-wheeler," said the middle brother.

و قَالَ الْأَخُ الْأَوْسَطُ: "حَتَّى أَنَّكَ لَا تُجِيدُ رُكُوبَ دَرَّاجَةٍ ذَاتِ عَجَلَتَيْنِ."

"I'm not small!" shouted Jimmy. "I can do everything you can!"

فَصَرَخَ جِيمِي قَائِلًا :"أَنَا لَسْتُ صَغِيرًا! أَسْتَطِيعُ فِعْلَ أَيِّ شَيْءٍ بِإِمْكَانِكُمَا فِعْلُهُ !"

He ran to his brothers and grabbed one of the bicycles. "Just watch!" he said.

ثُمَّ رَكَضَ نَحْوَ أَخَوَيْهِ و أَمْسَكَ بِإِحْدَى الدَّرَّاجَتَيْنِ و قَالَ:" فَقَطْ شَاهِدَانِي! "

"Be careful!" yelled his oldest brother, but Jimmy didn't listen.

فَصَاحَ أَخُوهُ الْأَكْبَرُ: "انْتَبِهْ!"، و لَكِنَّ جِيمِي تَجَاهَلَهُ.

Throwing one leg over, he tried to climb the large bike. At that moment, he lost his balance and crashed on the ground, directly into a mud puddle.

حَاوَلَ جِيمِي أَنْ يَرْكَبَ الدَّرَّاجَةَ الْكَبِيرَةَ فَرَمَى بِرِجْلِهِ ، و لَكِنَّهُ فَقَدَ تَوَازُنَهُ و سَقَطَ عَلَى الْأَرْضِ فِي بِرْكَةِ وَحْلٍ.

His two older brothers burst out laughing.

فَانْفَجَرَ شَقِيقَاهُ الْأَكْبَرَانِ ضَاحِكَيْنِ.

Jimmy jumped on his feet and wiped his muddy hands on his dirty pants.

اِنْتَفَضَ جِيمِي وَاقِفًا و مَسَحَ يَدَيْهِ الْمُلَطَّخَتَيْنِ بِالطِّينِ عَلَى سِرْوَالِهِ الْمُتَّسِخِ.

This just caused his brothers to laugh more.

و هَذَا مَا جَعَلَ أَخَوَيْهِ يَضْحَكَانِ أَكْثَرَ.

"Sorry, Jimmy," said the oldest brother in between laughter. "It's just too funny."

قَالَ الْأَخُ الْأَكْبَرُ مُقَهْقِهًا:" أَنَا آسِفٌ يَا جِيمِي، و لَكِنَّ هَذَا مُضْحِكٌ جِدًّا."

Jimmy couldn't stand it anymore. He kicked the bike and ran home with tears streaming down his face.

لَمْ يَسْتَطِعْ "جِيمِي" تَحَمُّلَ سُخْرِيَتِهِمَا أَكْثَرَ، فَرَكَلَ الدَّرَّاجَةَ وَهَرَعَ نَحْوَ الْبَيْتِ وَدُمُوعُهُ تَتَسَاقَطُ عَلَى خَدَّيْهِ.

Dad watched his sons from the backyard. He closed his book and went towards Jimmy.

شَاهَدَ اَلْأَبُ أَبْنَاءَهُ مِنْ فِنَاءِ الْبَيْتِ، فَأَغْلَقَ كِتَابَهُ وَلَحِقَ بِجِيمِي.

"Honey, what happened?" he asked.

سَأَلَ الْأَبُ:" مَاذَا حَدَثَ يَا عَزِيزِي؟"

"Nothing," grumbled Jimmy. He tried to wipe away his tears with his dirty hands, but instead he smudged his face even more.

فَأَجَابَ جِيمِي مُتَذَمِّرًا:" لَا شَيْءَ."و حَاوَلَ أَنْ يَمْسَحَ دُمُوعَهُ بِيَدَيْهِ الْمُتَّسِخَتَيْنِ، و لَكِنَّهُ لَطَّخَ وَجْهَهُ أَكْثَر.

Dad smiled and said quietly, "I know what can make you laugh..."

فَابْتَسَمَ الْأَبُ و قَالَ بِهُدُوءٍ: "أَنَا أَعْرِفُ الشَّيْءَ الَّذِي يُضْحِكُكَ."

"Nothing can make me laugh now," said Jimmy, crossing his arms.

فَقَالَ جِيمِي جَامِعًا يَدَيْه:" لَا يُمْكِنُ لِأَي شَيْءٍ أَنْ يُضْحِكَنِي الْآنَ."

"Are you sure?" said Dad and began to tickle Jimmy until he smiled.

فَسَأَلَ الْأَبُ: "هَلْ أَنْتَ مُتَأَكِّدٌ؟" و بَدَأَ بِدَغْدَغَةِ جِيمِي حَتَّى ابْتَسَمَ.

Then he tickled him so much that Jimmy started giggling.

و اسْتَمَرَّ الْأَبُ فِي دَغْدَغَةِ جِيمِي بِشِدَّةٍ إِلَى أَنْ بَدَأَ يَضْحَكُ.

They rolled on the grass, tickling each other until they both laughed loudly.

و تَدَحْرَجَ الاثْنَانِ عَلَى الْعُشْبِ يُدَغْدِغَانِ بَعْضَهُمَا الْبَعْضَ إِلَى أَنْ تَعَالَتْ قَهْقَهَاتُهُمَا.

Still hiccupping from his hysterical laughter, Jimmy jumped on Dad's lap and hugged him tight.

اِرْتَمَى جِيمِي فِي حُضْنِ وَالِدِهِ وَ عَانَقَهُ بِحَرَارَةٍ وَ هُوَ مَازَالَ يُحَوْزِقُ مِنْ شِدَّةِ الضَّحِكِ.

"I was watching you ride your bike," said Dad, hugging him back.

قَالَ الْأَبُ مُعَانِقًا اِبْنَهُ الصَّغِيرَ:" كُنْتُ أُشَاهِدُكَ و أَنْتَ تَقُودُ دَرَّاجَتَكَ."

"And I think you're ready to ride a two-wheeler."

"أَعْتَقِدُ أَنَّكَ مُسْتَعِدٌّ لِقِيَادَةِ دَرَّاجَةٍ ذَاتُ عَجَلَتَيْنِ الْآنَ."

Jimmy's eyes sparkled with excitement. He jumped on his feet. "Really? Can we start now? Please, please, Daddy!"

تَحَمَّسَ جِيمِي و لَمَعَتْ عَيْنَاهُ، فَانْتَفَضَ وَاقِفًا و هُوَ يَقُولُ: "أَحَقًّا مَا تَقُولُ؟ هَلْ يُمْكِنُنَا أَنْ نَبْدَأَ الْآنَ؟ أَرْجُوكَ يَا أَبِي، فَلْنَبْدَأِ الْآنَ!"

"Now you need to take a bath," said Dad smiling.
"We can start practicing first thing tomorrow morning."

فَأَجابَ الْأَبُ مُبْتَسِمًا:
"يَجِبُ أَنْ تَأْخُذَ حَمَامًا الْآنَ،
سَنَبْدَأُ التَّدْرِيبَ غَدًا."

After a long bath and a family dinner, Jimmy went to bed. That night he could barely sleep.

بَعْدَ حَمَّامٍ طَوِيلٍ و عَشَاءٍ مَعَ الْأُسْرَةِ، ذَهَبَ جِيمِي إِلَى فِرَاشِهِ، و لَمْ يَتَمَكَّنْ مِنَ النَّوْمِ مِنْ شِدَّةِ حَمَاسِهِ.

He woke up again and again to check if it was morning.

و كَانَ يَسْتَيْقِظُ مِرَارًا و تِكْرَارًا لِيَتَأَكَّدَ مِنْ حُلُولِ الصَّبَاحِ.

As soon as the sun rose, Jimmy ran to his parents' bedroom.

و عِنْدَمَا أَشْرَقَتِ الشَّمْسُ، أَسْرَعَ جِيمِي إِلَى غُرْفَةِ وَالِدَيْهِ.

Jimmy tiptoed towards their bed and gave his father a little shake. Dad just turned to the other side and continued snoring peacefully.

مَشَى جِيمِي بِهُدُوءٍ نَحْوَ سَرِيرِهِمَا ثُمَّ هَزَّ وَالِدَهُ هَزَّةً خَفِيفَةً، و لَكِنَّ الْأَبَ الْتَفَتَ إِلَى الْجِهَةِ الْأُخْرَى و وَاصَلَ شَخِيرَهُ في اطْمِئْنَانٍ و سَكِينَةٍ.

"Daddy, we need to go," Jimmy murmured and pulled off his covers.

هَمَسَ جِيمِي:"أَبِي، عَلَيْنَا أَنْ نَذْهَبَ."

Dad jumped and his eyes flew open. "Ah? What? I'm ready!"

قَفَزَ الْأَبُ مِنْ مَكَانِهِ قَائِلًا:" آهٍ؟ مَاذَا؟ أَنَا جَاهِزٌ !"

"Shhhh..." whispered Jimmy. "Don't wake anybody."

فَهَمَسَ جِيمِي: "هس...لَا تُوقِظْ أَحَدًا."

While the rest of the family was still sleeping, they brushed their teeth and went out.

بَيْنَمَا كَانَ بَقِيَّةُ أَفْرَادِ الْأُسْرَةِ نَائِمِينَ، فَرَشَ الْأَبُ و الْأَرْنَبُ جِيمِي أَسْنَانَهُمَا و غَادَرَا الْبَيْتَ.

As he opened the door Jimmy saw his orange bike, sparkling in the sun. The training wheels were off.

و حِينَ فَتَحَ الْأَبُ الْبَابَ، رَأَى جِيمِي دَرَّاجَتَهُ الْبُرْتُقَالِيَّةَ تَشِعُّ تَحْتَ نُورِ الشَّمْسِ، و لَاحَظَ أَيْضًا أَنَّ عَجَلَتَيِ التَّدْرِيبِ قَدْ اخْتَفَتَا.

"Thank you, Daddy!" he shouted as he ran to his bike.

صَاحَ جِيمِي: "شُكْرًا لَكَ يَا أَبِي!" و ركَضَ نَحْوَ دَرَّاجَتِهِ.

Dad showed him how to mount it and how to pedal. "Let's have some fun!" Dad said, putting a helmet on Jimmy's head.

أَرَاهُ وَالِدُهُ كَيْفَ يَرْكَبُ الدَّرَّاجَةَ و يُدَوِّرُ الدَّوَّاسَاتِ، و قَالَ و هُوَ يَضَعُ الْخُوذَةَ عَلَى رَأْسِ جِيمِي: "فَلْنَمْرَحْ قَلِيلا."

Jimmy took a deep breath, but didn't move.
"Come on. I'll help you into the seat," Dad insisted.

أَخَذَ جِيمِي نَفَسًا طَوِيلًا و لَكِنَّهُ لَمْ يَتَحَرَّكْ، فَأَصَرَّ الْأَبُ قَائِلًا: "هَيَّا، سَأُسَاعِدُكَ عَلَى رُكُوبِ الدَّرَّاجَةِ."

"Umm..." mumbled Jimmy, his voice shaking.
"I'm...I'm scared. What if I fall again?"

فَتَمْتَمَ جِيمِي بِصَوْتٍ مُرْتَبِكٍ: "أَنَا....أَنَا خَائِفٌ، مَاذَا لَوْ سَقَطْتُ مُجَدَّدًا؟"

"Don't worry," reassured his dad. "I'll stay close to catch you if you fall."

فَطَمْأَنَهُ الْأَبُ: "لَا تَقْلَقْ، سَأَبْقَى قَرِيبًا مِنْكَ لِأُمْسِكَكَ إِذَا مَا سَقَطْتَ."

Jimmy hopped on his bike and began pedaling slowly.

قَفَزَ جِيمِي فَوْقَ دَرَّاجَتِهِ و حَرَّكَ الدَّوَاسَاتِ بِبُطْءٍ.

When the bike tipped to the right, Jimmy leaned to the left. When the bike tipped to the left, Jimmy leaned to the right.

اسْتَمَرَّ جِيمِي يَتَّكِئُ عَلَى الْجَانِبِ الْأَيْسَرِ حِينَ تَمِيلُ الدَّرَّاجَةُ إِلَى الْيَمِينِ، و يَتَّكِئُ عَلَى الْجَانِبِ الْأَيْمَنِ عِنْدَمَا تَمِيلُ إِلَى الْيَسَارِ.

Sometimes he fell down, but he didn't give up – he tried over and over again.

كَانَ يَسْقُطُ أَحْيَانًا، و لَكِنَّهُ لَمْ يَسْتَسْلِمْ، بَلِ اسْتَمَرَّ فِي الْمُحَاوَلَةِ.

Morning after morning they practiced together.

تَمَرَّنَ الْأَبُ و الْاِبْنُ مَعًا كُلَّ صَباحٍ.

Dad held on while Jimmy wobbled, and eventually the little bunny learned to pedal fast.

و كُلَّمَا ارْتَعَشَ جِيمي أَوْ تَمايَلَ، أَمْسَكَ بِهِ الْأَبُ، إِلَى أَنْ تَعَلَّمَ الْأَرْنَبُ الصَّغِيرُ أَخِيرًا كَيْفَ يَقُودُ بِسُرْعَةٍ.

Then one day Dad let go and Jimmy could ride all by himself without falling even once!

وفِي يَوْمٍ مِنَ الْأَيَّامِ، تَوَقَّفَ الْأَبُ عَنْ إِرْشادِ جِيمي، فَتَمَكَّنَ أَخِيرًا مِنْ الْقِيَادَةِ بِنَفْسِهِ دُونَ أَنْ يَسْقُطَ و لَوْ مَرَّةً!

Dad smiled. "Now that you know how to ride, you'll never forget it."

اِبْتَسَمَ الْأبُ و قَالَ: "لَقَدْ تَعَلَّمْتَ كَيْفَ تَقُودُ الدَّرَّاجَةَ الْآنَ، و لَنْ تَنْسَى ذَلِكَ أَبَدًا."

"And I can race too!" exclaimed Jimmy.

قَالَ جِيمِي مُتَعَجِّبًا: "و يُمْكِنُني أَنْ أَتَسَابَقَ أَيْضًا!"

That day Jimmy raced with brothers.

و فِي ذَلِكَ الْيَوْمِ، تَسَابَقَ جِيمِي مَعَ إِخْوَتِه.

Guess who won the race?

اِحْزِرْ مَنْ فَازَ فِي السِّبَاقِ!